NORSE MYTHOLOGY:
CAPTIVATING STORIES OF THE GODS, SAGAS AND HEROES

© **Copyright 2015**

All rights Reserved. No part of this book may be reproduced in any form without permission in writing from the author. Reviewers may quote brief passages in reviews.

Disclaimer

No part of this publication may be reproduced or transmitted in any form or by any means, mechanical or electronic, including photocopying or recording, or by any information storage and retrieval system, or transmitted by email without permission in writing from the publisher.

While all attempts have been made to verify the information provided in this publication, neither the author nor the publisher assumes any responsibility for errors, omissions or contrary interpretations of the subject matter herein.

This book is for entertainment purposes only. The views expressed are those of the author alone, and should not be taken as expert instruction or commands. The reader is responsible for his or her own actions.

Adherence to all applicable laws and regulations, including international, federal, state and local laws governing professional licensing, business practices, advertising and all other aspects of doing business in the US, Canada, UK or any other jurisdiction is the sole responsibility of the purchaser or reader.

Neither the author nor the publisher assumes any responsibility or liability whatsoever on the behalf of the purchaser or reader of these materials. Any perceived slight of any individual or organization is purely unintentional.

Contents

INTRODUCTION: SOURCES AND OVERVIEW 8

CHAPTER 1—NORSE CREATION STORY 11

ICE AGE CONTEXT 13

GODS OF DIFFERENT TYPES 14

OTHER "CREATURES" 15

THE END 20

GEOGRAPHY 20

CHAPTER 2—THE NINE REALMS 21

CHAPTER 3—GODS AND THE "GIANTS" OF JÖTUNHEIM 24

VANIR GODS AND GODDESSES 24

AESIR GODS AND ASYNJUR GODDESSES 27

THE JÖTNAR GIANTS AND COHORTS 30

CHAPTER 4—MIDGARD AND THE HUMANS 33

END OF THE GLACIATION 33

THE LAND EVOLVED INTO GREATER FERTILITY 35

NORDIC IRON AGE 37

VIKING PERIOD (800–1100 AD) 38

THE NORMANS 39

HEROES GO TO VALHALLA 39

TRUTH BEHIND THE MYTH? 40

CHAPTER 5—ELVES, DWARVES, TROLLS AND VALKYRIES 42

LUMINOUS ELVES 42

DARK DWARVES 43

SUPERNATURAL TROLLS 44

VALKYRIES—CHOOSERS OF THE FALLEN 45

CHAPTER 6—ODIN, FRIGG, THOR, AND LOKI 47

ODIN VISITS JÖTUNHEIM 47

FRIGG, MOTHER OF THE GODS 48

THOR, GOD OF THUNDER AND LIGHTNING 49

LOKI THE TRICKSTER 53

CHAPTER 7—THE DEATH OF BALDR 58

BALDR'S DEATH BY STURLUSON 58

BALDR'S DEATH BY SAXO GRAMMATICUS 63

SIMILARITIES AND DIFFERENCES IN THE TALES 64

CHAPTER 8—CONFLICT BETWEEN THE REALMS 65

RAMPANT SELFISHNESS 66

BINDING FENRIR 69

BINDING LOKI 71

RAGNARÖK—A TIME OF DOOM AND NEW BEGINNINGS 73

CHAPTER 9—ENGLISH DAYS OF THE WEEK 76

CHAPTER 10—POPULAR CULTURE AND NORSE MYTHOLOGY 78

CONCLUSION 81

Introduction: Sources and Overview

I want to thank you and commend you for reading the book, "Norse Mythology: Captivating Stories of the Gods, Sagas and Heroes".

This book gives an overview of Norse mythology, telling some of the stories of the gods, giants and other creatures of that lost era before history began.

Though the world came to know of the Norse and their legends through Roman interaction about the time of Christ, most of what we came to know was handed down from folk tales gathered by native writers like Snorri Sturluson (c. 1179–1241). This was from a time when the Norse had already been converted to Christianity. Some of what Sturluson wrote was clearly influenced by

Christian beliefs of the time. As with all sources, we have to assume at least a little bit of bias was involved. The age of belief in the Norse gods had ended. We can only guess how much of those old beliefs were left out because they may have been incompatible with the new beliefs of Christendom. Sturluson gathered the tales in a work now known as the *Prose Edda*.

Several anonymous writers of the pre-Christian era created poems which have collected in what is now called the *Poetic Edda*. These pre-date Sturluson's work and thus are far more likely to give us insights into the thinking and attitudes of the early Norse people.

Danish scholar Saxo Grammaticus gave us a Latin language version of Danish history, *Gesta Danorum,* written in the twelfth century. But even earlier, we have more matter-of-fact writing of Roman historian Tacitus in the first century, discussing the tribes of the region they called Germania.

As with most stories, it's best to start at the beginning. And as with any story of gods, we start with the Norse version of creation.

Chapter 1—Norse Creation Story

Like most cultures, the rugged folk of the North have their own myth of creation. For them, it started with Ymir, ancestor of all the giants of Jötunheim. Later, Odin and his two brothers, Vili and Vé, defeated Ymir and formed the world from the giant's carcass—hair for the trees, bones for the hills, blood for the ocean, skull for the heavens, brains for the clouds and eyebrows for the land of humans called Midgard (Middle Earth or Middle Land).

None of the stories are clear about the origins of the three Aesir gods—Odin and his brothers. In some respects, these three are similar to the Greek gods, the brothers Zeus, Poseidon and Hades, who defeated the Titans and replaced them as rulers of the universe.

The universe became a giant tree called Yggdrasil which grew out of a well called Urd. Within the tree's branches and roots resided the Nine Realms.

The name itself comes from Yggr—"The Terrible One"—a name frequently given to Odin. For the well, the name "Urd" meant "destiny."

Norse researcher, Daniel McCoy, describes the two places—Yggdrasil and Urd—as extensions of the Norsemen's concepts of time. The Well of Urd he depicts as a "reservoir of completed or ongoing actions that nourish the tree and influence its growth. Yggdrasil, in turn, corresponds to the present tense, that which is being actualized here and now."

Like many primitive cultures, time is seen as repeating cycles instead of unbounded and linear. The waters of the past seep into the tree, affecting its form. Eventually, this water gathers on the leaves, like the dew, and runs back into the well, thus creating a new present. Those who gain control over this flow are said to possess great magic, because they display "a greater degree of control over destiny."

In Norse philosophy, the power of free will and fate interact, and give birth to reality. Those who were created participate in the creation. To the Christian biblical literalist, such a viewpoint may seem strange and perhaps even blasphemous. But to researcher Rod

Martin, Jr., the notion of Christians being participants in creation is not so unusual. Christ told his followers, for instance, that each of them could do the miracles he did and even greater. Reading again the Bible's Genesis 1:26 with this knowledge in mind, the notion that God created His children to look like him takes on a new meaning—not as gods, but as "baby gods." In other words, the children of God are not yet mature, but fully capable of creating once they learn well their lessons.

Ice Age Context

A fact not well appreciated in our modern society is that we currently live in an Ice Age interglacial called the Holocene. All of the talk of "global warming" should be welcome news to us all, but somehow warmth has been turned into an evil villain. Norse mythology was borne out of an era of increasing warmth which had made civilization possible. Before then, ice had ruled the climate for something like 90,000 years, and threatens to do so again, today. But even as most of the world came to know agriculture, Norway, Denmark, Sweden, and Finland had remained largely buried in ice, at least for hundreds of years.

In their mythology, wild land surrounded civilized territory. In those uncivilized realms, deadly cold still ruled. It took hundreds of years to melt enough of the ice so that land was exposed for growing crops. Memories of those harsher times still persist in the legends. In fact, the earth itself is still adjusting from the end of the last glacial period of the current Ice Age—land today is still rising after being freed from the 90 millennia of continent-crushing, mile-high glaciers. In Sweden, for instance, an inland, coastal lake was once a bay, open to the ocean, only a few hundred years earlier. The land, once crushed by the ice, is still rebounding, albeit somewhat more slowly than the initial elastic bounce some twelve thousand years ago.

Gods of Different Types

First came the giants—wild, uncivilized, and powerful. We will see more of them in chapter 3.

The Vanir are another set of gods in Norse mythology. They are frequently associated with the indigenous folks of the northlands— the first people to fill the void left by the melting glaciers. Those original folk were later overcome by invading Indo-Europeans.

The Aesir gods are sometimes associated with the conquering invaders who overwhelmed and took in the original inhabitants as their subjects.

Other "Creatures"

Land spirits are powerful beings associated with localized areas of land. From all that was written about them, it's hard to draw a clear-cut line between them and the gods. In fact, the line separating land spirits from elves, giants and dwarves is equally as blurred.

The land spirits jealously guard the realms they oversee. They easily take offense when someone mistreats the land, and they dish out curses just as easily as blessings.

Elves are also powerful beings, frequently called "luminous." Freyr, a Vanir god, and honorary Aesir, also seemed to be associated with the elves of Alfheim, possibly even their ruler, for he lived there, instead of in Asgard or Vanaheim. Yet, in some writings the distinction between elves and gods seems clearer and more pronounced.

Dwarves, unlike the common word used in our language, were not short people. At least nothing in the writings of the Norsemen suggests any deficit in height. There was the suggestion of invisibility and perfectly black in appearance. Were they "invisible" because they were black and not easily seen at night? They called the underground of Svartalfheim their home—a place full of mining and forges. Many of the fine artifacts of civilization, used by both gods and men, were forged by these beings. These artifacts included Mjölnir (Thor's hammer), Skíðblaðnir (Skidbladnir: Freyr's ship with perpetual fair winds), Gungnir (Odin's spear), Gleipnir (the chain which bound evil Fenrir when everything else had failed), and many others. Dwarves don't merely like the darkness; if exposed to the sun's rays, they immediately turn to stone.

On occasion, dwarves have been labeled "black elves," so the line between dwarves and elves remains somewhat unclear, as well. Because of their skill with metals, it's easy to compare the Norse dwarves with the Cyclopes of Greek myth who fashioned great weapons for Zeus, Poseidon, and others. We cannot help but wonder if the Greeks and Norsemen were talking about the same group of people—blacksmiths who learned an ancient art that was lost and then learned again by the humans at a far later age.

The Norns were three females, each with more power over the path of destiny than any other individual in the universe. They made their home in the Well of Urd, below Yggdrasil. In some versions of myth, they controlled destiny by carving runic symbols into the trunk of the great tree. In other versions, they wove a great tapestry with each strand controlling the life of another. One of these females was named Urd (like the well itself), which comes from the word which means "what once was" in Old Norse. Another was called Verdandi ("what is coming into being"). And the last was called Skuld ("what shall be"). Unlike the Greek fates, the destiny woven by the Norns was much more malleable. It left room for brave individuals to change their own destiny.

Valkyries are the choosers of the fallen. They are female spiritual aides to Odin, who carry dead heroes to Valhalla—a sort of heaven for brave warriors. In more modern times, such as with Wagner's music—*Ride of the Valkyries*—these divine females have been made to look noble. But they have a darker side. They also choose who will be slain. In fact, they have been portrayed on numerous occasions as downright bloodthirsty. They are extensions of Odin, doing his bidding as if they were appendages of his.

Disir are female spirits who acted as guardians of specific individuals, groups, or places. The Valkyries were sometimes called Odin's Disir. And like the Valkyries, the Disir could be warlike in nature.

Ask and Embla were the first humans. When two tree trunks washed ashore onto the land which the gods had only recently raised from the ancient waters, Odin and his brothers gave them *önd* (breath or spirit), *óðr* (inspiration or ecstasy), and something called *lá* which has not to this day been translated. The two humans were given Midgard to rule. The man's name comes from Old Norse, *askr* ("ash tree") and the wife's name meant "water pot." Symbolically, these two names paralleled the functioning of Yggdrasil and Urd—the Great Tree and the Water Well of creation. This imagery emphasizes the fact that one cannot long exist without the other—Yggdrasil and Urd, man and woman.

Sleipnir was an eight-legged horse belonging to Odin. Upon Sleipnir, the chief god made his numerous trips up and down Yggdrasil to visit the Nine Realms, always searching for more knowledge. Sleipnir came into being after Loki had shape shifted into a mare and later became pregnant by a giant's stallion.

Hugin and Munin were two helping spirits in the form of ravens. Their names meant "thought" and "desire," respectively. As you might have guessed, these two high-flying eyes were helpers of Odin, keeping him informed about events far and wide. Like the Valkyries, Hugin and Munin were semi-autonomous, but also extensions of Odin himself.

Berserkers *(berserkir)* and Ulvhethnar *(úlfheðnar)* were two forms of warrior shamans, each with their own totem animal. Berserkers ("bear shirts") naturally chose the bear as their symbol. Ulvhethnar ("wolf hide"), on the other hand, chose the wolf as their icon. Both would go into battle, fearlessly not wearing armor or clothes—only an animal mask and pelts—and madly attacking the enemy with wild abandon. In fact, this is where we get the English word *berserk*. In the age of Vikings, Berserkers and Ulvhethnar would inevitably frighten their enemies by their insane actions. It was commonly believed that these warrior shamans would remain unharmed by both iron and fire. Certainly, a warrior's glee for battle would make many a defender timid, even if only for a few seconds. In battle, a few seconds is all that is needed to win in a one-on-one struggle.

The End

Unlike the Greek's and their mythology, the Norse had the end of times already figured out. Their "twilight of the gods" was called Ragnarök—a time when most of the gods would die, and the worlds would suffer greatly all manner of cataclysms. But because of their view of time and nature as cyclic, this big ending would also be a new beginning.

Geography

The realms were loosely divided into two key types—*innangard* and *utangard*. Innangard—"inside the fence"—was considered to include all lands which were law-abiding, orderly and civilized. Utangard—"outside the fence"—on the other hand, referred to realms which were rough, wild, ancient and chaotic.

Only Asgard and Midgard had names which contained the -gard suffix, and thus referred to fortified places of order, protected from the chaos. Asgard was the realm of the Aesir, while Midgard was the realm of humanity. We will see more of these two places and the other seven worlds in the next chapter.

Chapter 2—The Nine Realms

Odin (sometimes called Woden) would frequently take his stallion, Sleipnir, for a ride up and down Yggdrasil, visiting the Nine Realms. Besides Asgard, world of the Aesir gods, the other eight are,

- Midgard—the home of mankind. This was the middle world or "middle earth" amidst the Nine Realms.

- Vanaheim—the territory of Vanir gods. This was a place of wilderness, lawlessness and chaos, though perhaps not as much as some other realms. After the Aesir-Vanir war, these two bands of gods developed a far closer relationship. They not only exchanged hostages to strengthen their mutual bond, but there were indications that the Vanir goddess Freya was actually Frigg, Odin's wife.

- Jotunheim—land of the giants, a third group of powerful gods. These were frequently seen as enemies of humanity and the other gods, though there were exceptions. Loki, for instance, was an adopted brother of Thor, but frequently annoyed everyone with his tricks, pranks, and betrayals.

- Niflheim—primitive ice world.
- Muspelheim—primeval realm of fire.
- Alfheim—the realm of elves.
- Svartalfheim—the land of dwarves.
- Hel—the dominion of the goddess of the same name and realm of the dead, also called Helheim.

Each of these worlds, outside of the human's Midgard, had their manifestation in the tangible world of humankind. For instance, the invisible (to humans, at least) world of Jotunheim intersected with human wilderness. Hel connected to every graveyard.

The number nine held special significance to pre-Christian Germanic peoples—a group which included the Norsemen of Denmark, Sweden, Norway, and later Iceland. For instance, Odin hung from a tree for nine nights in a daring act of self-sacrifice as part of his quest for more knowledge. Heimdall, guardian of the Aesir, was born of nine mothers. And sacrificial feasts lasted for nine days.

Rudolf Simek, a philologist, suggested that this love of the number nine came from the fact that the lunar calendar was based on 27 days which is a multiple of nine. This, of course, was referring not to the synodic period (29 days, 12 hours, 44 minutes and 3 seconds), but to the sidereal month—the amount of time for the Moon to return to its same position against the background stars (27 days, 7 hours, 43 minutes and 12 seconds). Our modern use of the synodic month refers to the Moon returning to its same phase—from one New Moon to the next.

In the next chapter, we take a closer look at the giants and other gods.

Chapter 3—Gods and the "Giants" of Jötunheim

Like the Greeks and their Titans, the Norse have a special name for their primordial gods; today referred to as "giants," the more appropriate term might be "devourers." And like the Greeks and their Olympian gods, a younger group (Aesir gods) overthrew the older, coarser giants.

First, we will look at the Vanir gods—more refined than the giants, but not as sophisticated as the Aesir.

Vanir Gods and Goddesses

These gods normally lived in Vanaheim or called it their place of origin.

Njörd—He was the father of Freyr and Freya. Njörd's wife was one of the giants named Skadi. His responsibilities included the sea and fertility.

Freyr (also Frey)—An honorary member of the Aesir, originally of the Vanir. He was the god of sexual and agricultural fertility. He was frequently accompanied by his great boar, Gullinborsti ("Golden Bristled"). Though originally from Vanaheim, and a member of Asgard, his home was in Alfheim—land of the elves. A great deal of speculation has surrounded Freyr on this point of fact. Was he their king? An ally? The original texts never clarify this issue. Understandably, Freyr has slept with a great many goddesses and female giants. In fact, he had even slept with his own sister, Freya. Incest was taboo amongst the Germanic peoples, but apparently not amongst the Vanir.

Freya (also Freyja)—Like her brother, Freyr, she was an honorary member of the Aesir. Her husband's name was Odr. Because of the similarity in husband and wife names, a strong case has been made that Odr is none other than Odin, and that Freya is merely another name of Frigg, Odin's wife. Loki had accused her of having slept with all the gods, including her brother, and even some of the elves. She is a goddess of fertility, love, beauty and elegant property. If she had lived today, she might even be called the "party girl" of the gods. She wielded great power—the *seidr*—manipulating the prosperity, health and desires of others. Amongst her many powers is the ability to shape shift into the form of a falcon.

Nanna—In some versions, she was the wife of the Aesir god, Baldr; in others, she spurned Baldr and married the human named Hoder. In the text of *Gesta Danorum*, Nanna was merely the mortal daughter of King Gevar. In Snorri Sturluson's writings, she was the daughter of Nepr, one of Odin's sons. So, this would make her Odin's granddaughter, and Baldr's niece. In such case, she would be pure Aesir, and not Vanir. And as Baldr's wife and niece, incest would also be a part of the behavior in Asgard. Like so many myths of the ancient past, conflicting versions make it difficult to keep the gods and goddesses straight.

Hoenir—Originally, he was an Aesir god, but after the truce of the Aesir-Vanir war, he was given to the Vanir as a hostage. The few stories about him seem to portray him as a bumbling idiot. When the Vanir consulted him, Hoenir would always get his answers from the giant, Mímir, a source of great wisdom. When Mímir was unavailable, Hoenir would merely mumble some ambiguous reply. In the *Prose Edda,* Hoenir is ironically mentioned as the source of humanity's ability to reason. In another work, the *Gylfaginning,* humanity's sources of reason are Vili and Vé, Odin's two brothers. Could Hoenir merely have been another name for one of Odin's brothers? According to still another source, the *Völuspá*, Hoenir would be one of the few gods to survive Ragnarök—the end of their current world and the beginning of the next.

Aesir Gods and Asynjur Goddesses

Aesir is more properly the male term for the gods of Asgard, and Asynjur is the female term. For our own convenience, we will refer to both as Aesir. The following gods called Asgard "home":

Odin—He was king of the gods, a position held in other pantheons by the likes of Zeus and Jupiter.

Frigg—She was the wife of Odin. As we've already seen, she may well be from Vanaheim, originally known by the name Freya.

Thor—He was one of the sons of Odin. This was the god of thunder and storms, and a fierce warrior who carried a hammer called Mjölnir, fashioned for him by the dwarves.

Loki—An adopted giant of Jötnar, son of Odin. He was a trickster, frequently causing trouble in Asgard and elsewhere.

Heimdall—This god could see and hear with such clarity, Odin set him to guard the entrance to Asgard—where the great rainbow bridge, called the Bifrost, connected the home of the gods with the rest of the universe. He was said to have had nine mothers. He required far less rest than even a bird, so he rarely needed to leave his post. He could see for hundreds of kilometers during light and dark. And he could hear the grass grow. Asgard's enemies had little chance to slip past this god unnoticed.

Ullr—Was the son of the goddess Sif. He excelled in hunting, skating, skiing, and archery. According to Saxo Grammaticus, a Danish historian of the Middle Ages, Ullr took leadership over the gods during a period when Odin had been in exile. His name made its appearance in a number of solemn oaths, such as swearing by the "ring of Ullr," or the time when Odin swore the blessings of "Ullr and all the gods" to the person who might rescue him from between two fires.

Sif—Goddess of grain and wife of Thor. She was also the mother of Ullr, but it seemed the father was someone other than Thor, perhaps before Thor and Sif became husband and wife.

Bragi—This god was the official poet and minstrel of the Asgard court.

Idun—She was the wife of Bragi. This goddess dispensed a magical fruit which gave the gods their long life.

Baldr—A son of Odin and Frigg. In some versions, he was considered to be radiant and beloved by all the Aesir gods.

Höðr—His name meant simply, "warrior," and there was not much mentioned about him except as the one who had killed Baldr.

Forseti—His name meant "chairman." He was not mentioned very much in the old texts. One of the poems of the *Poetic Edda* mentioned that he settled disputes. Sturluson, in the *Prose Edda,* told us that Forseti was the son of Baldr and Nanna, a claim that at least one scholar disputes.

Vili and **Vé** —The two brothers of Odin, who helped slay the giant, Ymir, and to form the world with the giant's body. When Odin was on his many travels searching for wisdom, Frigg (Freya?) would grow lonely. One or the other of the brothers would keep her company, even at night.

Tyr—In the literature, he was a minor god and little was said about him. But there are so many strong references to him that it seems likely that the Viking Age believers had merely forgotten Tyr in favor of Odin. For instance, only Tyr was brave enough to risk his own hand in the mouth of Fenrir in order to bind him with a magic cord.

The Jötnar Giants and Cohorts

Jötnar is the plural form of jötunn—the giants of Jötunheim. The giants were frequently enemies of the humans and the Aesir gods. Though they are frequently referred to as giants in the literature, the original meaning of these creatures was "devourers."

Fenrir—A giant wolf and son of Loki and giantess Angrboda. He was the brother of Hel and Jormungand.

Hel—She was the goddess of Helheim—the underworld where the dead were kept. She was the daughter of Loki and Angrboda and thus the sister of Fenrir and Jormungand. Her name meant "hidden."

Jormungand—A giant serpent and son of Loki and giantess Angrboda. Accordingly, he was the brother of Fenrir and Hel. He circled the earth in the oceans of Midgard. In fact, he is frequently called the Midgard Serpent. His name means "great beast." He and Thor were destined to slay each other in Ragnarök.

Skadi—A giantess who loved the mountains where the snow never melts. She was considered to have been a great huntress with bow and snowshoes. She had been married to the Vanir god, Njörd, with whom she produced two children—Freyr and Freya. And if Freya was another name for Frigg, then Skadi was the grandmother of Baldr.

Surt—His name meant "black" in Old Norse. He was a fire giant who spent a great deal of time in Muspelheim—the realm of fire. His favorite weapon was a burning sword.

Nidhogg—One of the preeminent serpents beneath the Yggdrasil world-tree. There, he and his fellow dragons would eat at the roots of the tree, causing great damage. This threatened all Nine Realms. His name meant "he who strikes with malice." Though he did not live in Jötunheim, he is certainly associated with their efforts to pull the cosmos back into chaos.

Skoll and Hati—Two wolves which forever chased the Sun and the Moon in order to devour them.

Aegir and Ran—These two were husband and wife, respectively. They lived in a great hall underneath the ocean. In fact, Aegir's name meant "ocean" while his wife's name meant "robber." Aegir was usually shown as a congenial host. His wife however, was frequently seen drowning luckless sailors and pulling them down to her underwater world. The couple had nine daughters. Of all the giants, these two seemed to have the friendliest relationship with the Aesir gods, quite often inviting them to feast with them.

Garm—A great wolf who fought the god Tyr during Ragnarök. There is some evidence that Garm is merely another name for Fenrir.

In the next chapter, we return from the realm of the gods to the place we call home.

Chapter 4—Midgard and the Humans

This was the realm of tangible reality, not that the realms of the gods and giants were not real. They were real to the Norsemen, but in a different way, perhaps in the same way that gravity and time are real, yet invisible.

End of the Glaciation

For thousands of years, the ice had been melting. Sea levels had been steadily rising throughout this period. In fact, from the depths of the last glacial period of the current Ice Age (~18,000 BC), sea level had risen 110 meters (360 feet). Except for a brief, 1,300-year cold period, called the Younger Dryas (~10,900–9620 BC), global warming continued to make the environment of the northern lands more and more hospitable.

From about 9000–6000 BC, the Maglemosian culture settled in southern part of what is now called Scandinavia. During this period of time, oceans rose roughly 40–50 meters (131–164 feet) from the melting ice. Early in this period, Great Britain was connected to continental Europe, and what is today Denmark was connected to southern Sweden. For several thousand years a freshwater lake (Ancylus Lake), somewhat larger than today's Baltic Sea, stood behind that land bridge. The combination of post-glacial rebound lifting the land and sea levels rising changed the coastlines markedly. A vast area southwest of Scandinavia stood above water in what is now the southern portion of the North Sea. That prehistoric area is now called Doggerland by today's scientists, and was about the same size as the British Isles.

By about 8000 BC, the entire coastline of Norway had been freed of ice. Stone age settlements filtered in, taking advantage of fishing, sealing and hunting opportunities.

The 3000-year period of the Maglemosian people saw them dwelling in wetland and forest environments. Their hunting and fishing tools were made of flint, bone, and wood. Homes were constructed of bark and their domestic tools were made from bone, flint, and horn.

The Land Evolved into Greater Fertility

Gradually, over this period, tundra turned to grassland and then became dotted with trees. Life found the warmer land and filled it. As more of the ice melted and sea levels rose, the Maglemosian culture gradually disappeared, replaced by the Kongemose culture (6000–5200 BC).

For the Kongemose, their economy was founded upon hunting wild boar, roe deer, and red dear. Also, they added fishing from coastal areas.

To the north of the Kongemose people lived the Nøstvet and Lihult people. Existing in open settlements, the Nøstvet people (6200–3200 BC) used stone age axes made from rocks like quartzite, quartz, and flint. For sustenance, they hunted marine mammals and seafowl, as well as gathering and fishing. Over time, their settlements grew in size, indicating that their populations were growing and more easily supported by a sedentary standard of living. Petroglyphs of this and other cultures dotted the land of prehistoric Sweden as early as 5000 BC, showing drawings of reindeer, bears, elk and seals.

In the southern part of Scandinavia, the Kongemose were replaced with the Ertebølle culture (5300–3950 BC). These newcomers were a hunter-gatherer culture which also used fishing and pottery making.

Still later, the Funnelbeaker culture (4300–2800 BC) gradually replaced the Ertebølle in southern Scandinavia, and also their northern neighbors, the Nøstvet and Lihult cultures, bringing farming and animal husbandry to the region.

According to the Kurgan hypothesis, this group called by modern scientists, "Funnelbeaker," was considered to have been a non-Indo-European culture. This was what Marija Gimbutas called "Old Europe"—the peoples later overtaken by the Indo-Europeans of Central and West Asia. The Funnelbeaker group gave way to the intrusion of what has been called the Corded Ware culture—an extension of the Yamna (or Yamnaya) culture.

The Corded Ware culture (2900–2350 BC) brought Indo-European language to the area. They covered a much larger area, including most of habitable Scandinavia, Germany, parts of Russia and the northern parts of Eastern Europe. This new culture greatly influenced the language of the region, but did not entirely replace it.

Belgian scholar, Edgar Polomé (1920–2000), former professor of comparative religions and languages at the University of Texas, assessed the influence of Corded Ware on the indigenous peoples of Europe in the 3rd millennium BC. According to him, roughly thirty percent of the non-Indo-European basis found in the modern German language comes from the language of the Funnelbeaker culture, native to the southern portion of Scandinavia.

From about 1500 BC—the Nordic Bronze Age in Denmark—the peoples of the area buried their dead alongside worldly artifacts, in burial mounds. Numerous bronze artifacts from this period attest to the social stratification into classes. Artifacts included many religious items and even musical instruments.

Nordic Iron Age

From the 4th to the 1st century BC—what we might also call the Pre-Roman Iron Age—the climate took a turn for the worse in southern Scandinavia (including Denmark). It became wetter and cooler, greatly limiting agriculture. Ironically, in today's world, global warming is seen as evil, but quite the opposite is true. Cold is the real killer, and it forced people to migrate southward into Germania, creating problems at the Roman frontier.

This was the beginning of the Norse Iron Age, because people of the region began to remove iron from the ore found in peat-bogs.

During the period from the 1st century to the fifth century AD, the Roman empire maintained relations with the Danish isles and Jutland. The Romans even suggested that the Danes could become a "client state" of the empire, but this proposed relationship, of course, never materialized. Even so, there was some evidence that some members of the Danish warrior elite had joined the Roman military.

Viking Period (800–1100 AD)

The Vikings were not only fierce warriors, but they were fearless explorers and relentless merchants. Their travels took them to England and Ireland (creating settlements 793–820 AD), deep into what is today Russia (854 AD) and the Caspian Sea (creating a large settlement 880 AD), through the Black Sea (settlement at Miklagard, 839 AD), through Old Byzantium, to Spain (844 AD), to Italy

(860 AD), conquering Normandy (911 AD), all across Northern Europe, to Iceland (874 AD), Greenland (982 AD) and Vinland, North America (1000 AD).

Over the next thousand years, the borders of the Scandinavian countries fluctuated greatly. The Norse became Christians gradually and sometimes painfully.

The Normans

The Normans (Norse men) were conquerors from Norway, Denmark, and Iceland. In the 10th century, they subjugated the land in northwest France called Normandy. Then, they conquered parts of Italy in the early 11th century. They also captured Sicily and Malta from the Saracens. Because of their fierce fighting reputation, Norman mercenaries fought throughout the Mediterranean. They took England in 1066 with the Norman invasion of William the Conqueror. So, the nobility and language of England was forever changed and influenced by the Vikings.

Heroes Go to Valhalla

In the dim, prehistoric times before Ragnarök, the Valkyries, as extensions of Odin's will, took only the strongest and most heroic warriors fallen in battle, to Valhalla. There, the warriors would hone their skills and prepare themselves for the coming of Ragnarök. In this, Odin was being selfish, for he wanted to thwart prophecy by preparing an overwhelming human army of the very best to hold off the giants and their forces of chaos in those final days.

Truth Behind the Myth?

Many researchers have long wondered what truths there may be behind the myths of old. How much was pure fiction? How much was based on fact, perhaps misunderstood by a primitive people who heard them. Perhaps those primitives did not have sufficient vocabulary to understand the original stories which possibly now are lost forever. As I suggested in my book, *Greek Mythology: Captivating Stories of the Ancient Olympians and Titans,* some old stories may well be based on fact. They may merely need to be looked at from the right perspective to gain the greatest possible understanding. Though such an approach does not provide perfect answers, it may provide a method by which we can speculate on possible meanings. These, in turn, may lead us to other clues we may not otherwise have considered.

Behind the wall of lost knowledge, there lies a truth that may yet be discovered.

In the next chapter, we take a brief look at some of the others living in the universe of Norse mythology, including elves, dwarves and the Valkyries.

Chapter 5—Elves, Dwarves, Trolls and Valkyries

Luminous Elves

The elves were considered to be luminous beings, close to nature. They were said to have been "more beautiful than the sun." They were forever being associated with the Vanir and Aesir gods in the poetry of Old English and Old Norse.

Like so much of Norse mythology, the defining separation between gods, dwarves, elves and land spirits was unclear. Perhaps such logical details were unimportant to the Vikings and their forebears. There may well have been a great deal of overlap between the groups. But elves seemed to have a far stronger link to the Vanir gods. For instance, Freyr lived in Alfheim and may well have been their lord. There was even one piece of Old Norse poetry which over and over again referred to the Vanir as elves.

Yet, there were other sources which made clearer distinctions between Vanir and elves, making them seem entirely separate.

Elves could cause illness and could as easily heal. They had the ability to mate with humans and their children possessed great intuition and magic.

Dark Dwarves

Norse mythology brought us a far different image of dwarves than we have seen in the literature of others. They were not short. But they were pitch-black in color. Like the stories of Tolkien, the Norse dwarves lived underground and loved to mine metals and other precious things from the ground. Svartalfheim was their home. This other world was focused only on the labyrinth of caves and mines underground. Did anything ever happen above ground there?

As in other myths, Norse dwarves were skilled smiths in the various metals and excellent craftspeople. Besides Thor's hammer, Freyr's ship, Odin's spear and ring, and Sif's long, golden hair, the dwarves created many other wondrous tools and artifacts. They fashioned the lightweight chain, Gleipnir, with which the gods were finally able to bind Fenrir the wolf.

They also created a magnificent necklace named Brisingamen which Freya wore on occasion.

Dwarves were extremely intelligent and used powerful magic. Despite their power, they remained vulnerable to the sun's rays. If exposed to sunlight, they immediately turned to stone.

The dwarves were also extremely strong. Four of them—Austri, Vestri, Nordri and Sudri—were said to hold up the four corners of the sky.

Supernatural Trolls

Originally, in Norse mythology, trolls may have been merely a derogatory term for the Jötnar—the giants of Jötunheim. They were often pictured as living in caves, mountains or detached rocks. Later, in the old stories of Scandinavia, trolls took on a different image—always living far from humans. They were thought to have been dangerous, dimwitted, and ugly. Peculiar landmarks were sometimes explained as that of troll turned to stone by being exposed to the sunlight, much as the dwarves were transformed by strong light.

One old Scandinavian belief told that trolls were frightened away by lightning. This may merely have been an echoing of the tales where Thor fought against the Jötnar with his lightning hammer.

When the region became Christianized, trolls were said to have become frightened by the church bells, sometimes destroying entire churches by throwing huge stones at them.

Valkyries—Choosers of the Fallen

The Valkyries were, in some ways, like angels on the battlefield, helping the selfless heroes who had died there to find their way to Valhalla—the hall of the fallen heroes. But in the original Norse tales, these noble maidens seemed more like sinister witches. They not only chose who amongst the fallen would go to Valhalla, but they frequently chose who was to die. Quite often, they would use cruel magic to ensure their wishes were met.

Before to the Battle of Clontarf, for instance, twelve Valkyries sat, like the Norns, weaving at their looms the destiny of the warriors who were about to fight. Instead of thread, they used intestines. For weights, they used detached heads. For beaters, they used arrows and swords. Throughout their ritualistic weaving, they would sing their objectives with menacing glee.

To the Anglo-Saxons, their version of Valkyries (Old English, *wœcyrie*) were viewed as female spirits of bloodshed and massacre.

The Valkyries' primary task was to bring worthy warriors to Valhalla so that their training could continue. Since the warriors were already dead, their practice could be deadly in every normal sense, but the warriors would be completely healed before the next day's practice.

Today, Valhalla is frequently pictured in Asgard, but there seems to be nothing in the literature to suggest this. Norse researcher, Daniel McCoy found clues in the Eddas and old place names that suggested Valhalla was always a part of Helheim—perhaps a special place there, separate from the other dead.

When the final battle was to come at Ragnarök, these human dead would fight on the side of Odin against the giants.

In the next chapter, we will focus on the four main characters of Norse mythology—Odin, Frigg, Thor, and Loki.

Chapter 6—Odin, Frigg, Thor, and Loki

Odin Visits Jötunheim

As king of the gods, Odin was obligated to know more than anyone else about the events of the Nine Realms. Because of this, he took frequent trips up and down Yggdrasil to gain more knowledge. One source of great wisdom was said to be Mímir's well. Drinking of its waters would give anyone superior knowledge. Mímir's well was located in Jötunheim, under the second root of Yggdrasil.

Because the giants were enemies of the Aesir, Mímir would not willingly give up the water without some compensation. Odin ultimately traded one of his eyes for a sip of the powerful water. And this is how the king of the gods came to be blind on one side.

From this, it remains curious that Mímir would choose to visit Vanaheim, on occasion, and assist Hoenir in his decisions.

Frigg, Mother of the Gods

Late in the history of Norse mythology, Freya and Frigg were separate goddesses, but even then, they shared a great many traits in common.

The name Freya meant merely "lady," which is a title instead of a proper name. As a word, it is similar to German *Frau,* which is very much like the English word "Mrs." Frigg, on the other hand, comes from the word meaning "beloved."

Both of them were experts as a *völva*—a practitioner of the magic known to them as seidr. With that magic, they could read and alter the web of destiny. Both Freya and Frigg possessed falcon feathers with which to transform into a bird. Such a skill would prove quite handy when the need arose for escape or reconnaissance.

Freya's husband was named Odr, and Frigg's husband was named Odin. In Old Norse, Óðr has the meaning of "ecstasy, furor, inspiration." Óðinn is simply the same word with a masculine ending.

The *Prose Edda* mentions Odr only briefly, saying that he was frequently away on long trips. It says that Freya was often found to be shedding tears of red gold because her husband was away.

Many of the Norse tales describing Odin talk of his long trips away from Asgard, journeying throughout the Nine Realms in order to gain more wisdom. So, even Freya's husband looks like Frigg's husband in many ways.

Both Freya and Frigg were accused of being unfaithful to their husbands. Frigg supposedly slept with a slave. While Odin was exiled from Asgard, his two brothers, Vili and Ve were left in charge. They did more than preside over the realm; in addition, they each frequently lay with Frigg until Odin could return home. In the *Poetic Edda,* for instance, Loki accused Freya of having lain with all of the elves and gods, which would have included Freyr, her own brother.

Because these two share so much in common, it seems highly likely that they were originally the same goddess who was named Frigg and sometimes called "lady" ("Freya").

Thor, God of Thunder and Lightning

His name was Þórr, in Old Norse. According to Vladimir Orel, in his handbook on Germanic etymology, in Proto-Germanic, the name was estimated to have come from Þunraz ("thunder").

Thor was the epitome of the courageous warrior. Every Viking warrior wanted to be like him. Besides his magical hammer, Mjölnir ("lightning"), Thor owned an unnamed belt which gave him double his normal strength. This thunder god could be seen frequently riding across the sky in his chariot drawn by goats.

Though Thor's father was Odin, his mother was a giantess who went by the names Jord, Hlöðyn, and Fjörgyn. So the modern retellings of Thor where he calls Frigg his mother are not entirely accurate; Frigg was to him only a stepmother.

In Midgard (Earth), humans often called upon Thor and his hammer to consecrate weddings and homes. The hammer was seen not only as an instrument of slaying evil, but of offering blessings. In a very real sense, these two functions were really one; both were actions of purification.

No one could blame Thor for being upset, then, when one day he woke up to find that Mjölnir was missing. How anyone could have gotten by Heimdall in order to carry out the theft was never explained.

In order to get the gods' primary instrument of protection back, Freya lent her falcon feathers to Thor and Loki so that the hammer could be found. Loki, already skilled at changing his shape, took the feathers and flew directly to the likeliest suspects in Jötunheim.

Upon Loki's arrival there, he returned to his more human-like god form and confronted the chief giant, Thrym ("noisy"), about the missing hammer. Thrym bragged that indeed he had taken the prize and had buried it deep in the ground. His ransom demand was that Freya marry him.

After Loki had flown back to Asgard, his report alarmed all of the gods, in particular Freya. Accordingly, the gods gathered to discuss their options. Heimdall suggested that Thor go to Jötunheim disguised as Freya. By pretending to go through with the wedding, Thor could reclaim Mjölnir and slay the thieves and their cohorts.

Thor feared that by dressing up as a woman he would become the laughing stock of all Nine Realms. To him, such a thing was not only dishonorable, but unmanly. Everyone in Asgard would mock him.

Ironically logical, for a change, Loki made the point that if they did not retrieve the hammer, Asgard could very well be ruled by giants. How much mocking would Thor receive under those circumstances? Grudgingly, Thor agreed to Heimdall's plan.

No expense was spared in preparing Thor's wedding dress. And Loki was dressed as the thunder god's maid-servant.

When the pair arrived in Jötunheim, Thrym boasted to his fellow giants that the gods had finally come to their senses and rewarded the chief giant with the honor he was due.

At the pre-wedding feast, Thor forgot his role and ate far too much for a dainty bride. He consumed not only an entire ox, but also eight salmon, and all of the petite delights which had been prepared for the other women. Not only that, he drank several barrels of mead.

Thrym was understandably suspicious. Never before had he seen a fair goddess with such an appetite. Cunning Loki replied, "The fair goddess has been so lovesick for you, that she hasn't been able to eat for a week."

Nodding in acceptance, Thrym was suddenly overcome with desire to kiss his bride-to-be. Pulling back Thor's veil, Thrym was confronted by Thor's threatening eyes.

"Never," said Thrym, "have I seen a maiden with such frightfully piercing eyes!"

Again, Loki's quick wit helped him devise a proper response. He told the giant that Freya had also been incapable of sleeping, because of her intense longing for him.

Now, Thrym was in a hurry to get to the ceremony. As with all weddings, Thor's hammer was needed to bless the marital ritual. Thrym immediately called forth the hammer. Moments later, Mjölnir lay in Thor's lap and the thunder god grabbed its short handle. First, he exterminated Thrym and then all of the wedding guests.

After he returned to Asgard, Thor felt gratified to change back into his normal attire.

Loki the Trickster

Loki was the Norse god of mischief. He also performed many heroic tasks, but only as a result of repairing the mischief he had already caused. He was sometimes associated with fire. In regard to these characteristics, he can be compared to the Greek god, Prometheus, for that Titan gave humanity fire and was forever provoking Zeus with pranks and tricks. And like Prometheus, Loki was ultimately bound up and forced to endure repeated suffering. This was to keep him from committing any more mischief. Prometheus had been bound up and forced to endure an eagle eating his liver by day, only to have the liver regenerate overnight, and to have the same torture repeated every day thereafter.

What had Loki done that was so bad? Here are a few examples.

Thor's wife, Sif, had long and flowing golden hair. One day, when Loki was feeling particularly bored, he cut off Sif's hair. Naturally, this enraged her husband, Thor.

The storm god threatened to kill the trickster, but wily Loki convinced him to spare his life if he could find an even finer head of hair for Sif. Loki suggested that he might be able to convince the dwarves of Svartalfheim to fashion a far more beautiful head of hair for Thor's wife.

Deep within the caverns of Svartalfheim, Loki talked to the dwarf Ivaldi whose sons fashioned for Sif a new head of hair more fine than the one she'd had. But they also created two other marvels. One was the finest ship in existence, created from thin slats of wood. This ship would always encounter favorable winds. Not only that, it could be folded up and tucked away in the owner's pocket. This ship was given the name Skidbladnir. The third gift was the deadliest of spears, called Gungnir.

Loki, overcome with mischievous delight, decided to stay a bit longer and to see if he could wrest more fun from this trip. He decided to ridicule two other dwarves, Brokkr and Sindri, telling them that they would never be able to forge three gifts as fine as those created by the sons of Ivaldi. Loki was so certain of their incompetence that he wagered his own head. Sindri and Bokkr took up Loki's challenge.

As always, Loki never played fairly. He shape-shifted into a fly and bit Sindri's hand. The assault was not enough to keep the dwarf from finishing a truly fine creation. Out from the fires, Sindri pulled a magical, golden-haired boar. He called his creation Gullinbursti ("golden bristled"). This boar shone brightly in the dark, excellent for leading its master at night. In addition, the boar could run through air, water, or land far better than any horse.

Next, Sindri placed another slab of gold on the fire. Brokker pumped the bellows to increase the fire's temperature. Suddenly, the fly bit Brokkr's neck, but this did not stop him from working the bellows. From the fire, Sindri pulled out a magical ring he called Draupnir. Every ninth night, Draupnir would give birth to eight golden rings of equal weight. Over time, this one ring could make any man or god extremely wealthy.

For the last gift, Sindri placed iron on his fire. He cautioned his co-worker that they both must be very careful for one mistake could prove costlier than all the gold they had used on the previous two gifts.

Desperate to foul the dwarves' work, Loki, as the fly, bit Brokkr on the eyelid. Blood flowed from the bite and prevented the dwarf from seeing what he was doing. But the two dwarves were such experts at what they did, that Loki's stings proved to be only an annoyance.

This last gift was to be Thor's hammer. They called it Mjölnir ("lightning"). This hammer would never miss its target. More than that, it would fly back into the owner's hand after each throw. The only flaw was that the handle was too short.

As the two dwarves prepared for their trip to Asgard to claim their wages, Loki arrived at the great hall before them. There he delivered the three gifts he had acquired. He gave to Thor the golden hair for his wife. To Freyr, he gave the ship and the golden boar.

When the dwarves arrived, Loki presented Thor with the hammer, and gave the spear and ring to Odin.

The gods were so pleased with their gifts that they had to agree that Loki owed the dwarves his head. To Loki's dismay, the dwarves approached the prankster with their knives ready. The former fly, ever so cunning, reminded them that he had promised his head, but not his neck. As the two dwarves prepared to return home to their forge, they happily sewed Loki's mouth shut so his cunning tongue could bother them no more.

How Loki ever got his head back was not clear, but this story was not the end of him.

The following account takes on the turning point in Norse mythology. This is where Loki goes too far and incites another to kill the beloved son of Odin and Frigg—Baldr.

Chapter 7—The Death of Baldr

There are two main versions of this story—one from medieval Icelander Snorri Sturluson, and the other from Saxo Grammaticus, in his *Gesta Danorum* ("history of the Danes").

Baldr's Death by Sturluson

Snorri Sturluson pictured Baldr as a generous, beloved, joyful, charming, courageous and innocent victim. It seems that Baldr gladdened the hearts of any and all who might spend time with him. The story of his death began with Baldr's dreams. Those visions from sleep foretold of his own demise. Young Baldr told his parents about his dreams.

Immediately, Odin took his faithful steed, Sleipnir, and rode to the underworld to confer with one of the dead—a seeress who had been quite skilled and wise about such things in life. In one of his many disguises, Odin arrived at the underworld puzzled to find preparations for a great feast underway. When he found the seeress, he asked her about the festivity. She told him that an exalted guest of honor was soon to arrive—the great god Baldr. Quite happily, she told how Baldr was to be killed. But suddenly, she stopped. The traveler who had awoken her seemed distraught. And just as suddenly, she realized that she had been telling Odin himself about his son.

Naturally, Baldr's mother, Frigg, became worried by Baldr's dreams and the preparations being made in the underworld. To protect her son, she combed the world for any potential threat and received from them each an oath that they would never hurt her son.

The other gods, ever in the mood for some rowdy sport, took advantage of Baldr's new situation. Each of them took turns throwing rocks, sticks and other objects at Baldr only to laugh as those objects bounced harmlessly off of their fellow god.

Loki saw this as an opportunity to have some evil fun. With his talent for shape shifting, he disguised himself and went to Frigg to inquire about what she had done to protect her son. "Did all things swear oaths to spare Baldr from harm?" he asked.

"Oh, yes," Frigg replied, "everything except the mistletoe. But the mistletoe is so small and innocent a thing that I felt it superfluous to ask it for an oath. What harm could it do to my son?"

Upon learning of this vulnerability, Loki found some mistletoe and returned it to where his adopted brothers were enjoying their latest pastime. The trickster found the blind god, Hodr, and stated, "You must feel quite left out, having to sit back here away from the merriment, not being given a chance to show Baldr the honor of proving his invincibility."

Hodr nodded in agreement. "Yes, but there is a good reason for that."

Loki held out his spear made of mistletoe. "Here. I will point your hand in the direction where Baldr stands, and you throw this branch at him."

So Hodr hurled the mistletoe spear, piercing Baldr and killing him instantly.

All of the gods stood in shock. They knew from what the seeress had told Odin, that this event would be the first sign that Ragnarök was on its way.

When Frigg's grief had subsided enough for her to speak, she asked for a volunteer to go to the underworld to offer a ransom to Hel for Baldr's release.

One of Odin's lesser-known sons, Hermod, agreed to take on the task. The god king offered Sleipnir to take Hermod on his journey, and away they went, carrying the hopes of all the gods for Baldr's rescue.

Baldr's funeral became a lavish affair. They outfitted Baldr's ship, Hringhorni, as a funeral pyre fit for royalty. But even the funeral did not go as planned. Baldr's ship became stuck and all of the gods working together could not dislodge it. They called for the giantess Hyrrokkin to help them. When she arrived, she gave the ship such a powerful shove that the land quivered.

As Baldr's dead body was lain to rest on the ship, his wife, Nanna immediately died of grief, and she, too, was placed on the ship next to her husband. When the flames had been lit, Thor used his great hammer to consecrate them.

All manner of gods, elves, dwarves, giants, Valkyries and others were assembled to see Baldr's ship as it disappeared in the distance.

Far from Asgard, Hermod spent nine nights riding through increasingly darker and deeper canyons to ransom that part of Baldr which had been condemned to Hel. When he found himself at the Gjöll ("roaring") river, the giantess Móðguðr confronted him to determine his purpose. It was her responsibility to let only those who were authorized to cross the bridge into Helheim.

When Hermod arrived in Hel's realm, he found Baldr placed in the seat of honor at the banquet Hel had thrown for him. The next morning, Hermod pleaded with Hel to release his brother. He told of all the sorrow experienced by the gods and other living things now that Baldr was no longer with them.

"If this is so," replied Hel, "then let everyone in the universe weep for him. When that happens, I will send him back to you. But if anyone refuses, he will remain here with me."

Upon Hermod's return to Asgard, messengers were sent to all the worlds to carry the news he had brought from Hel. Every creature did weep for Baldr except for the giantess Tokk ("thanks"). Unbeknownst to all, she was actually Loki in disguise. Tokk replied to the messengers, "Let Hel hold what she has!"

Later, Hodr was killed by a being named Vali, who it seems may have been created for this one purpose.

Baldr's Death by Saxo Grammaticus

The other version of the tale of Baldr's death is not as rich with details. And some of the details which were used are decidedly different.

For one thing, Hodr was not blind. And his name, which means "warrior," was more in keeping with his personality.

Both Baldr and Hodr were each great military leaders. They assembled their armies against one another all for the love of the beautiful Nanna.

Before the fight, Baldr had eaten an extraordinary and unique food which gave him invincibility. Hodr had found out about this. He knew he needed something which would level the field of battle. For this, he traveled for several days to the underworld and finally found a weapon with the right magical qualities to overcome Baldr's defenses.

During the battle, Hodr wounded Baldr, and Odin's son died several days later of his wounds. Despite the win, Hodr was later killed by an avenger named "Bous."

Similarities and Differences in the Tales

Both tales contain enough similarities to help us realize that there may have been a common and real event behind both of these stories.

And there were some striking differences. Both Baldr and Hodr have conspicuously different characters. Instead of the mild, likable fellow in Sturluson's version, Baldr is a brutal warrior who will stop at nothing to win in battle. The same thing can be said of Hodr. In this tale, he is no longer the blind victim of Loki's cruel entertainment, but an equally cunning warrior.

It is quite likely that both stories leave out critical details. Ultimately, we may never know the truth behind the myth.

In the next chapter, we look at some of the conflicts which make the mythical stories so much more interesting. A story without conflict, after all, is not much of a story.

Chapter 8—Conflict Between the Realms

It seems funny sometimes that we humans crave conflict. If a story is devoid of quarrels or fighting, it proves boring to most audiences. What would Roman conquest have been like if every tribe encountered merely said, "Sure, we would love to serve Rome. How much tribute do you want?" History would not have been as interesting to most people. If a motion picture were to be made without any conflict, it would certainly lose money, because people would tell their friends how awful it was. A good story requires that some good individual or group struggles against the bad. It has always been this way.

Life on the edge of the wilderness was not easy. Acquiring sufficient food was sometimes more than a little difficult. If one tribe ran out, through mismanagement or natural disaster, they might want to steal from another tribe nearby. Those who made a habit of stealing learned to enjoy conquest and power over others. These became the chieftains and later kings and emperors. A few of them were relatively benign and enriched humanity with their wisdom. Most were petty thugs who only took and never gave.

The idea of stealing from others has been with us for as long as humans have been self-concerned—pretty much forever. Odin and his three brothers attacked Ymir and built a new world from his giant carcass. The other devourers ("giants") did not like these intruders and their selfishness.

The Vanir gods were peaceful agrarians, for the most part. They were each responsible for one or another aspect of fertility. The Aesir gods were considerably more warlike.

Rampant Selfishness

Freya, a Vanir goddess, was a skilled magician who could alter the course of destiny. She was an accomplished practitioner in the art of seidr. Like the human practitioners of Old Northern Europe, she went from town to town, earning her keep with her talents. When, finally, she reached Asgard, using the name Heidr ("bright"), she became a favorite amongst the Aesir gods. Like some new drug, the gods found themselves greedily lusting after more and more of her services. This witch's magic, however, was corrupting their morals. They were losing control by giving into their basest desires. They were turning away from honor, obedience and kin loyalty in order to have more of her powerful work.

Rather than take responsibility for their own shortcomings, the Aesir gods ended up blaming Freya. They called her "Gullveig" ("gold greed") and sought to murder her for tempting them so thoroughly. Thrice they burned her alive, and thrice she rose from her own ashes like the phoenix of Greek mythology.

The Aesir treachery made the Vanir gods fear and hate them. Not long afterward, these bad feelings erupted into war. Each side in this Aesir-Vanir war used the talents they had in abundance. The Aesir used brute force and weapons of every kind. The Vanir, on the other hand, used magic of every imaginable sort. Both sides suffered, and each side alternately gained the upper hand, eventually losing it to their enemy.

With such an evenly matched conflict, and no end in sight, both sides became tired of the perpetual assaults and counter-assaults. Eventually, they called a truce.

The ancient Norse culture and that of the other Germanic peoples proscribed that each side should pay tribute to the other. The customary tribute included hostages to live amongst the other's tribe.

Freya, her brother Freyr and their father, Njörd, of the Vanir went to the Aesir. Hoenir and Mímir went to the Vanir.

In some tales, Mímir is a giant who lived under the great world-tree, Yggdrasil, jealously guarding his well of knowledge. But here, Mímir is Aesir and a valuable part of the trade. As in the other stories, Mímir possesses great wisdom.

Hoenir also seemed to have great wisdom, but only when Mímir was around. When the Vanir discovered that Hoenir was an idiot, they felt betrayed. Ironically, though, they cut off Mímir's head and sent it back to Asgard. Why they killed the source of wisdom, instead of the pretender, Hoenir, remains a mystery.

In Asgard, Odin used his own magic to preserve Mímir's head. From then on, he frequently consulted the bodiless head for advice.

Despite this breakdown in civility, gross misunderstanding, and misguided reaction, both sides were still weary of war. Instead of resuming hostilities, each god came together to spit in a sacred cauldron. Together, their spittle formed an entirely new creature called Kvasir—the wisest being of all time. Through this new being, their mutual pledge of harmony was kept.

Binding Fenrir

One of the sons of Loki was the fearsome wolf Fenrir. All three of his children by the giantess Angrboda were huge and threatening. And each one of them was ultimately banished to a location where they could do little harm. Hel was sent to the underworld to guard the dead. They tossed Jomungand into the oceans of Midgard. At first, however, the gods felt it best to keep the young wolf pup nearby so they could keep a watchful eye on it. To their surprise, however, Fenrir grew in size at a frightening pace. Very soon, they all had changed their mind. Allowing the wolf to roam free in Asgard would likely have led to devastation.

The gods of Asgard attempted to bind Fenrir with one chain after another. With each attempt, they received the wolf's permission with the lie that these were merely tests of the wolf's strength. To keep up the ruse, the gods would clap and cheer each time Fenrir easily broke free.

In desperation, the gods dispatched a messenger to the realm of the dwarves. As the foremost craftsmen, they should be able to produce a chain capable of keeping the great wolf bound. These ingenious dwarves of Svartalfheim forged a chain the strength of which even Fenrir could not overcome.

They crafted the chain from several ingredients: the beard of a woman, the roots of stones, the breath of a fish, the sound of a cat's footsteps, and the spittle of a bird. Because these are things which do not exist, struggling against them would prove futile. This clever creation of theirs they called Gleipnir ("open").

When Fenrir saw Gleipnir, he grew suspicious. This chain was not like the others in any way. It was strangely supple and light and the wolf suspected some kind of deception. At the gods' insistence, Fenrir assented on the condition that one of the gods or goddesses put their hand in his mouth as a show of good faith.

At first, no one dared do this. This grave risk was dangerous in two ways. First, it meant the certain loss of a hand. The intention was to bind Fenrir. If it worked, Fenrir would retaliate by chomping off the hand of the luckless god who might agree to do such a thing. Second, anyone who pledged on their honor that the intention with the chain was one merely of testing Fenrir's strength would be seen as a liar and oath-breaker. Both of these were reasons for great shame and marks of incompetence. Who would follow a god into battle who could not properly wield a broadsword? And who would follow a god whose oath could not be trusted?

The god Tyr saw the moral ambiguity of this predicament. He realized that if no one met this challenge, then they would all be guilty of cowardice and of allowing a wild beast to wreck havoc on their world. His was a brave self-sacrifice when he stepped forward and assured Fenrir that their intentions were honorable. He placed his hand in Fenrir's mouth, and promptly, the other gods bound the creature. When Fenrir could not break free, he bit down and severed Tyr's hand.

Binding Loki

After Loki had orchestrated Baldr's death and prevented his release from Helheim, he grew bolder in his disdain for his adopted brethren.

He had never been liked much for all the harm he had done in the past. More often, his actions had been burdensome rather than helpful. When Loki began insulting the other gods at every occasion, his welcome was worn exceedingly thin. Finally, all the Aesir gods agreed to capture him, but Loki discovered their plans.

He escaped and traveled far from Asgard. At a distant mountain, he built a house with a door on each wall so he could see the approach from each direction. During the day, he swam in the stream as a salmon and found a remote spot under a waterfall. At night, he would weave a net for fishing so he would have something to eat.

Odin saw where Loki had gone, but before the gods could get there, Loki threw his net in the fire and returned to the stream as a salmon. Even so, the prankster god had left too many clues. The other gods deduced that Loki had changed himself into a fish and fashioned their own net. A number of times they cast their net into the stream, but Loki barely escaped. Then, Loki, feeling crowded by the gods, took one desperate leap downstream so he might escape to the sea. But Thor, with his quick reflexes, snatched the fish in mid-air.

From there, the gods took Loki in his human-like form to a cave. There, they brought two of Loki's minor sons and forced one into the form of a wolf which promptly attacked the other son, drawing out his entrails onto the floor of the cave. From the entrails, the gods fashioned chains which were turned to iron. Giantess Skadi placed a venomous snake on the rock above Loki's head. From there it dripped poison onto the trickster god's face. But Sigyn, Loki's faithful wife, took a seat by his side holding a bowl to catch the venom before it could strike her husband. Yet, when the bowl became full, Sigyn had to leave in order to empty it. Each time venom struck Loki's face, he would thrash violently and this would cause earthquakes in Midgard.

Ragnarök—A Time of Doom and New Beginnings

A great deal of ill will had developed between the Aesir gods and Loki's family. His daughter, Hel, had refused to release Baldr from her realm in the underworld. Both of his sons, Jormungand and Fenrir had made nuisances of themselves, threatening the stability of the Nine Realms.

But when Ragnarök arrived, both Loki and Fenrir broke free of their bounds, and Jormungand broke free from the oceans of Midgard.

Surt was a fire giant from Muspelheim and he led the way against the Aesir and Vanir gods. Behind him were thousands of giants and other creatures of chaos.

Nidhogg, one of the great serpents which had gnawed at the roots of Yggdrasil, flew out from under the great World-Tree to come to the giants' aid.

Heimdall saw the approaching army of giants and sounded the alarm. Up from Valhalla, the army of dead heroes swarmed to Asgard's aid.

Wielding his burning sword, Surt cut through the sky and mountains with ease. He ended up fighting Freyr and, in the end, they killed each other.

Jormungand, the great Midgard Serpent, and one of Loki's sons, battled with Thor and they killed each other.

Fenrir devoured Odin, king of the Norse gods.

Next, the story of Ragnarök told that Tyr was killed by a great wolf named Garm. But because Tyr had tricked Fenrir into being bound, it seems that Garm may have been another name for Fenrir. The great wolf killed Tyr, and then was himself killed by Vidar, one of Odin's sons.

Two other wolves—Skoll and Hati—who had chased Sol and Mani (sun and moon) in vain for eons, now had their hopes renewed for devouring the heavenly bodies. At Ragnarök, these two caught their victims and the sky grew dark.

Heimdall and Loki battled and slew one another.

Afterward, the world sank into utter darkness and silence. Then, gradually the land and light returned as Baldr returned from Helheim. A new man and woman, Lif and Lifthrasir—both humans—took their first breaths in a newly green world. And ultimately, the gods returned and continued their joyful merrymaking.

The following chapters brings us back to the present, relating how Norse mythology has influenced our culture. First, we look at the days of the week.

Chapter 9—English Days of the Week

In the English language, the days of the week remain a complicated mishmash of Norse, Roman and English names.

Sunday, of course, refers to the sun.

Monday is easy enough to parse. It celebrates the Moon. So, it is our Moon day.

Tuesday is where we turn to Norse traditions. This is Tiw's day. Tiw is the Old English version of Tyr, the god who had sacrificed his hand in order to trick Fenrir into being bound by the magic cord, Gleipnir.

Wednesday is more difficult to parse. This is Odin's day, based on one of his many alternate names—Woden. So, this is Woden's day, in the middle of the week—hump day—the high point.

Thursday, of course, is easy. This is Thor's day—for the god of thunder, lightening and storms.

Friday is Freya's day or Frigg's day.

Saturday is the Roman contribution to the lot. This is Saturn's day—Roman god of the harvest, equivalent to the Greek Cronus. It's interesting to note that in Spanish, the day is called *sabado,* or Sabbath.

In the last chapter, we see how popular culture has been enriched with Norse mythology.

Chapter 10—Popular Culture and Norse Mythology

In the mid-to-late 1800s, German composer Richard Wagner created *Der Ring des Nibelungen,* a four-opera cycle which celebrated Norse mythology. The *Ring* cycle included:

- *Das Rheingold (The Rhinegold)*
- *Die Walküre (The Valkyrie)*
- *Sigfried*
- *Götterdämmerung (Twilight of the Gods)*

Ignatius L. Donnelly (1831–1901), a US congressman from 1863–1869, wrote a book on Ragnarök—*Ragnarök: The Age of Fire and Gravel* (1883)—after the success of his book, *Atlantis: The Antediluvian World* (1882). In it, he suggested that a great comet had struck our world about 10,000 BC, destroying an advanced civilization which had existed before then.

In 1954, science fiction writer, Poul Anderson wrote *The Broken Sword,* a story which featured a great many Norse gods, trolls and elves.

J.R.R. Tolkien's works of fantasy, *The Hobbit, The Lord of the Rings* (1955) and *The Silmarillion* (1977), were heavily influenced by Norse mythology, including magical runes, dwarves, elves, and trolls.

In 1962, comic book readers were treated to a new hero called Thor. Stan Lee, Larry Lieber and Jack Kirby's recreation of the ancient Norse god became a mainstay of comic book fans for decades. Later, their version of the god of thunder found his way into the movies with *Thor* (2011), *The Avengers* (2012), *Thor: The Dark World* (2013) and *Avengers: Age of Ultron* (2015). A new addition to this series is already in the works, called, *Thor: Ragnarok* (2017).

In the late 60s, science fiction writer, John Dalmas created a future Norse mythology with his story, "The Yngling." Several books have followed in that same universe.

The *Stargate* television series frequently featured a race of aliens called the Asgard, one of whom was named Thor. A small faction of the Asgard were called the Vanir.

Even the Harry Potter books of J. K. Rowling included references to Norse mythology, like the Death Eater Thorfinn Rowle, and werewolf Fenrir Greyback.

In 2014, a science fiction anthology by Carl Martin called, *Entropy's Children,* included a tale of historical science fiction about Odin who had been known as a young boy by the name of Olen Efel-Tosk. The story took place in the prehistoric era after the melting of most of the ice from Northern Europe.

Television's *Game of Thrones* also has Norse influences in its fictional world.

There are hundreds of other examples, too many to include in this small book. But it remains clear that the Norse gods are here to stay. Their influence has not died.

Conclusion

I hope this book was able to help you to appreciate and enjoy the rich stories of Norse mythology.

If you merely wanted an overview of this rich heritage, then you're done. But if you want a far more in-depth picture of Norse mythology, the next step might be to see if your local college offers courses in the subject. Naturally, there are many websites online, but use their information with caution. Some of them are incomplete and perhaps even misleading.

If you have enjoyed this book, please be sure to leave a review and a comment to let us know how we are doing so we can continue to bring you quality books.

Made in the USA
Middletown, DE
28 September 2016